Saved by Night

Haylie R. Beltran

DEDICATION

This book is dedicated to the
girl who saved me and all the
military couples out there
going through and or have
gone through long distance.
It's okay to not be okay.

CONTENTS

ACKNOWLEDGMENTS

I just want to say thank you Dani for choosing me as your person to experience life with. Also a huge thank you to all the people who helped me and gave me encouragement through this whole process. I would never be where I am today without you all. I want every reader who reads this to know that they are never alone.

COSMIC LOVE

Your Touch

Our hands meet slowly we open
up and interlock
Your arms wrap around me
Giving me the feeling of
being protected and secure.
I can feel your skin slowly
gracing mine.
My nerves take control.
My heart starts racing.
Slowly I try to focus on my
breathing.
So much is going on in the
background but you're the
only thing I focus on.
The only thing I feel…**YOUR
TOUCH**

Ceiling of squares

That Night you came home with
me
We counted how many squares
were on my ceiling
I Had no idea how you felt
about me or if you felt
anything at all
I just knew our two souls
clicked and became one
You later told me the Night
was the night you knew how
you felt about me.

Lilly

Flowers so beautiful, the
sunlight gives them life
You my love are my sunlight
You give me life in the love
you share
For you I will always grow,
letting me pedals open for
you.

Child of the universe

Stars in your eyes,
The moon in your heart,
You are the child of the Universe
Thus you rule over every star,
every planet, every comet, every
sky.
We live in your world
Your soul THE UNIVERSE…
I give everything to the universe
I bow down and let her rule over
me
As she is key for me to be happy
In her i trust, with everything
I let her guide me
For she is,
My eyes
My mind
My heart
Thus she is you, T
                        H
                         E
                          U
                           N
                            I
                             V
                              E
                               R
                                S
                                 E.

Thunderstorm

Daylight fades and the moon
gets blanketed by the gray
clouds.
A mid of silence then she
makes her presence known.
She strikes Just to show us
how beautiful she is,
splitting the colors of her
sky.

She creates the mystery of
herself constantly changing
her path, not letting anyone
know what's coming next.
Taking down her walls she
opens up.
She means no fear but instead
a safe place in the chaos of
the world.

My Love

My love it's you you that i
want
It's you that I need...
It's you that I need to
breath
It's you that I need to
survive
It's always you that's my
drive
Till the day I die

She did something to me
Now whenever I sleep
She's in my dream
Now she belongs all to
me

Moon

The Moon is so beautiful in
all of her phases: Waxing,
waning, half, and full.
She shares her beauty with
the light she shines.
The moon comes to soothe and
ease our minds.
She sees us when we cannot
see through.
She makes me see that I want
you.

Love

Though I'll never admit it I
have a weakness
LOVE…

Love is the name of my
weakness
Love has made me hurt
Love has made me cry

Always getting false hope so
why try?
I never had a reason to
Until I met you…

But why?
Why did I love?
Why did my heart choose you?

I guess that's an answer only
the universe will know, but
if i had to give an answer;
it would be that we were
meant to save each other
Well that's what it felt like

You have saved the meaning of
love for me
You have given me Love in
Unimaginable ways
You have loved me when i
haven't even loved myself
You have saved me from the
darkness

Please tell me she's real and I'm not dreaming.She is too perfect to not be fake.

Pizza Box Love

Something as simple as a box
of pizza
It was 11:30 pm and I hear a
knock at my door
A girl holding a box of
pizza?
You sent pizza to my house
because you knew I was
craving it
I open it to find a message
written inside the box
In big letters it spelt
I LOVE YOU
My stomach was filled with
butterflies
It was the most heartfelt
thing I had ever received
I was so happy over something
as simple as a box of pizza

Chance

In a field of roses she is a
lily
Standing above all
It was from the beginning I
knew I wanted her to be mine
Although i knew she could not
be
I knew that there was not
even a chance that she would
take a glance
So I ignored it and tried to
push the thought of her away

A month passed by and then
soon nine more did as well
Still she was who I thought
of everyday
Until I walked through that
door and I saw her sitting
there
That was all i needed the
Universe giving me my sign

Time

It was our time…
Our time to fall in love, so
we did exactly that
It started off slow with just
simple text then simple text
turned into texting every
second of the day
With every text you sent you
took a piece of my heart,
with it growing the craving
of your love.

Her love is mine

Wall of flowers

A wall of beautiful flowers
Filled with your love that
showers
I sit and stare at them for
hours
Yet simply their beauty never
overpowers
Just a wall of beautiful
flowers

Say her name and watch
as my soul leaves my
body to find her.

HER

She looks into my eyes, so i
look back into hers
I feel a sense of strength
yet weakness at the same time
Thus I know she is my
greatest strength yet my
greatest weakness
I know that with her I have
the strength to do anything
imaginable but would simply
die over the thought of
losing her
HER
It's just simply her
It's always going to be her…
She's My everything…My Night

.

Shooting Star

You caught my eye
So bright yet not lit up?
I felt as though i was
dreaming
I was not…it's reality
You my star came into my
arms
I could not hide the fact
that i was beaming
How could I be so lucky?
You were
A star
A dream
A fairytale
You my star lit me up, so I
did the same for you
Giving each other the light
we so desperately needed
You turned me into the star I
used to be
Bright, Happy, and shining
Now I rest with you my star
Side by side in our forever
home THE SKY

The most intense
feeling your soul will
ever feel.

-Love

Mesmerized

I'm Lost in your love
Mesmerized by the electricity
of your touch and the
intensity of your kisses
Completely and utterly in
love with you.

Say I love you

The day that will forever be
indented in my memories
I knew what you were trying
to say but I wanted you to
tell me
I wanted to hear it come out
of your mouth
Then you said it
Hearing it felt like my heart
was being serenaded to my
favorite love song
My heart D
            R
          O
           P
            P
             E
              D.
A mid of silence then
appeared the biggest smile on
my face.
I love you too.

The first time I saw
you, My entire being
lit its fire.

-Twin Flame

Night

Lost in your beautiful eyes I
fall to my knees
I would do anything you need
Without you having to ever
say please
For you are my weakness
Like a star placement you are
my Venus
I give you my love with ease
And to you I am the only
thing your heart sees

I would give everything
to you in a heartbeat.
Even if that means
myself.

-Devotion

Late Night Drive

Nothing beats late night
drives with the person you're
in love with
Two in love souls surrounded
by the sky
Blasting music until they
feel alive
Just staring into each others
eyes
Heart stopping really
Just driving around the city
Because everyone knows
everything at night is
pretty

"To love and to cherish, Till death do us part".

-Forever

When I First Knew I Loved You

I first knew from when we laid in my bed and counted how many squares were on my ceiling.

I knew from when in the beginning you were willing to risk everything just to see me.

I knew from when I first kissed your lips sitting in your passengers seat, both clueless on what would happen that night.

I knew from when I stood in front of you at your car door listening to you nervously try to find the words to tell me that you Love me for the first time.

I knew I was so deeply in love with you when you asked

me if we could go see him
together.

I knew I would love you
forever when you had me in
your arms and stared at his
picture then told me I had
his eyes.

At that moment…
The only thing I saw was you
The only thing I felt was
your touch
The only thing I heard was
him telling me You're
perfect.

Black hole

Saved by Night

NOVEMBER 15

Last Call

November 15 12:03 am
You called me for the last
time
My eyes hurt from how hard I
had been crying
I laid in bed drowning myself
in my tears
Knowing it would be months
until I got to hear your
voice again
Since that moment it's felt
as though you died and so my
heart did to

Remember we are always
under the same moon.

-Night

Saying Goodbye

It's not goodbye
It's never goodbye
It's always i'll see you
later or i'll see you soon
We promised never to say
goodbye because we'll always
see each other again
It could be
Days
Weeks
Months
And even Years till we meet
again, but we know we'll
always come home

I've never loved anyone
the way I have loved
you
At first it scared me,
but now I have taken
down my wall that is
the protector of my
emotions
And have let you in
I am no longer afraid
but now open to every
possibility with you.

Again

I was so vulnerable
So selfish to think it was
finally my time
Finally the wake up called i
needed
I let myself fall so deep
So unguarded
I'm not hurt just mad at
myself

Physically and mentally suffering.

-Pain

Hurt

I laid in my cold pitch black
room screaming
Blasting *Teen Romance* By Lil
Peep
I swear my neighbors could
hear it to
I never imagined this is what
i'd go through
I HATE IT
Constantly in a state of blue
I'd do anything just to see
you
I cried and screamed so much
that night my body ached for
days

If I died today. Would you save me anyway?

Distant Love

2,000 miles has never felt so
far until now
I can no longer hold your
hand and it's tearing me up
inside
I miss you
I want you to come home
Though I know you cannot
I selfishly want you to drop
everything just to come see
me
But if I asked you to do
that, what kind of partner
would I be?
So instead we choose Distant
Love.

Desperately in love
with you, and I just
want to be with you
constantly.

-Pining

Twilight

I've never understood that
scene in *Twilight*
When Edward left Bella, and
Bella sat in that chair in
the same spot and the same
clothes for three months, but
i do now
In this case you are Edward
and I am Bella
I felt her pain if not worse
For 13 weeks I hurt on a
different level
Constantly just going through
the motion of life but not
actually living it

Who Knew love would hurt?

Your Voice

Your voice…
I would know your voice from
a mile away
I would know your voice all
the way to outer space
Your voice is my home
I close my eyes and dream of
it everyday
Your voice is the whole
universe to my world
Oh what i'd do to hear your
voice Every morning, Every
afternoon, and Every night

Self Vs. Self. The
battle you'll never
win.

The Battle Continues

I think I'm at a point in my
battle where giving up sounds
like a prize, but I know that
giving up will never solve
any of the struggles.
So what is the point?
Maybe I tell myself that it
will stop the pain or that it
will make things better
But deep down I know that's
false
I feel better lying to myself
than breaking the news to
myself that in reality there
is no end to this.

Guilt

I sat in bed discussed with myself
Guilt radiating throughout my body
How could I be happy when you're experiencing pain everyday?
How can I laugh when they have made you forget how your own laugh sounds?
How can I do anything without feeling guilty?

My heart is gold and
everyone is a miner
digging and hitting.
Slowly breaking my
heart apart

You My Love

It's you that i see in every
pretty view
It's you that i hear in every
single song
When I lay my head to rest at
night

I dream of my future with
you,
Longing to feel your touch
because with you is where I
belong
You are my world my light

Forever is what is true
My love for you is oh so
strong
Constantly you stay on my
mind Night.

I'm Lost without you.

Depression

I laid in bed almost everyday
Not because I wanted to but
because I couldn't move
I drowned myself in my own
sadness
Just hoping I would save
myself
I DIDN'T
I let myself greave
I let myself breath
And yet it was still there
That horrible feeling that
one that never goes away

Your Smile

Your smile is forever on my
mind
So beautiful, so bright, so
kind
I could stare at it for
hours
It's like looking at a field
of flowers
So hypnotizing yet it calms
That damn smile…Oh my the
shit i'd do for that smile

Wherever you go Jupiter will follow!

Scale

Anxiously standing on the
scale waiting for the numbers
to stop
I couldn't believe what I saw
It had only been two weeks
and my weight was decreasing
faster than I could keep up.
Food grossed me out I
couldn't bring myself to eat
I was too sad to even think
about food
So instead I didn't
Watching my body changed
scared me, but i couldn't
help it
I tried
I ate
But even when I ate the
biggest meal of my life
I still lost more weight

My body was the warning signs but my mind and heart ignored them as if they were never there.

Emotionless

Straight face tearless eyes
but instead all there is, is
pain
I am the "strong one"
I am not allowed to feel sad
nor anxious or even scared
The only thing i'm allowed to
be is okay
My body is forever stuck on
putting on a smile
When in all it's a lie
I am never strong behind
closed doors
Dying inside with the weight
of holding back what I
actually feel
Lost in the fumes of my
tragic fire
With eyes that arc tired from
holding back all the tears

With You

I don't want to call you
I don't want to FaceTime you
I want to be with you
To feel your touch
To hear you say I Love You
To see your breathtaking
smile
To smell your perfume when I
hug you
To taste our love again
I want to be with you

Alone

I hate feeling alone
It's the absolute worse
feeling
To be all by yourself
I lose it
I can't help but to feed into
the voices telling me i'm no
one
Maybe they're right
Maybe this whole time
My whole life has been a lie

You can sleep away all
your pain but it's
still going to be there
when you wake up

-avoiding

Lie

They told me "You'll be fine"
LIARS
What a lie that came to be
They lied because they were
scared
They were scared because they
had never seen me cry
They were scared because for
once in my life I showed
weakness

Forever

If forever means never ending
That is what I wan't
Constant love that is always
extending
That is what I wan't
I promise i'll stay
In your arms i'll lay
You're always my forever
And forever i'm your Always

How could I continue to
live if what I was
living for is gone

Promise

With every kiss I promise…
With every hug I promise…
With every word I promise…
I want you forever
Baby please
If forever is what we have
Will you promise to be mine?

All the pain

All the hurt

There will soon be an end.

About the Author

I initially started to write poetry as a way to express how I was feeling because I couldn't do it through talking.As years went by poetry just became my life. I was always writing poetry ,and When my partner left for the military I used poetry as a way for our love to stay connected and to ease the pain of her being away. Poetry has given me so much and through this book I hope that I was able to share that with you.